William Nicholson: Painter

Landscape and Still Life

Towner Art Gallery, Eastbourne 1995

Published in association with the exhibition

William Nicholson: Painter
Landscape and Still Life

Organised by the Towner Art Gallery, Eastbourne.

Exhibition tour:-

Towner Art Gallery, Eastbourne	4 November – 31 December 1995
Kettle's Yard, Cambridge	6 January – 25 February 1996
Nottingham Castle Museum	2 March – 28 April 1996
Browse & Darby, London	2 May – 1 June 1996

Exhibition organised by Penny Johnson.
Assisted by Kate Fowle, Anthony Davis and Emma Markland.

Catalogue designed by Kerry Tanner.
Typesetting by LDA Design & Advertising, Eastbourne.
Printed by Offset Colour Print, Southampton.

The catalogue has received support from the Paul Mellon Centre for Studies in British Art.

All paintings by William Nicholson have been reproduced by kind permission of Elizabeth Banks.

ISBN 1 871360 080

Front cover: *The Silver Casket* (cat.16) Private Collection

Contents

Acknowledgements

Penny Johnson, Curator

In the Sussex Downs William Nicholson (1872-1949) found a haven from the demands of painting society portraits in London. Here, and later elsewhere, he was able to develop the painting of landscapes and still lifes, subjects that appealed to him most as a painter. This is the first exhibition to focus on William Nicholson's paintings of these two subjects, which reveal his essential qualities as a painter.

As many of these paintings are in private hands, this exhibition would not have been possible without the interest and generous spirit of the owners. It is especially kind of them to lend paintings which are treasured possessions. In some cases the paintings have not been seen in public for more than fifty years. The exhibition selector, Hilary Lane and I would like to thank the lenders for the welcome that they gave us when we visited to see the pictures.

I am grateful to the following public collections for responding so positively to my request for loans:- The Arts Council Collection, Birmingham Museums & Art Gallery, Leeds City Art Gallery, Nottingham Castle Museum and Art Gallery, Sheffield City Art Galleries and the Tate Gallery.

In locating the whereabouts of the paintings, I was very fortunate in having the help and advice of William Darby of the Browse & Darby Gallery, London. I am indebted to him for his co-operation throughout the preparation of the exhibition and for introducing us to the William Nicholson Trust, who kindly gave access to their archive.

Elizabeth Banks, the artist's daughter and a Trustee of the William Nicholson Trust, has not only provided a foreword to this catalogue but has assisted at every stage with her helpful and perceptive advice. I thank her for giving permission to reproduce her father's paintings in the catalogue and in connection with the exhibition.

I was delighted that Lillian Browse, a friend of William Nicholson and author of the major monograph on the artist, agreed to write a memoir for the catalogue. I would like to thank her warmly for this; her knowledge of the artist and his work was also invaluable in the early stages of the exhibition.

The William Nicholson Trust introduced us to Patricia Reed, who is compiling a catalogue raisonné of Nicholson's work. I am most grateful to her for her expertise and contribution to the catalogue, an essay about the career of William Nicholson, the chronology and the bibliography.

I was very pleased that four contemporary painters agreed to write a response to William Nicholson's work. Each directs our attention to different qualities in the paintings. I would like to thank Patrick Caulfield, Patrick George, Merlin James and Isobel Johnstone for their thoughtful and illuminating pieces.

Many people have helped with the preparation of this exhibition. Particular thanks are due to Suzy van den Berg, Clare Cecil, Bettie Clark, Catherine Clement, Jill Constantine, Jane Farringdon, Anne Goodchild, Michael Harrison, Richenda Hobson, Linda Homfray, David Ker, Matt Pia, Alex Robertson, Nicholas Serota, Tessa Sidey, Evelyn Silber, Elizabeth Smallwood, Kate Stoddart, Neil Walker, Kerry Tanner and the staff of the Towner Art Gallery.

Financial assistance has been received for the exhibition from a number of sources, to whom I am most grateful. The Arts Council of England awarded the Towner a Development Grant in order to research the exhibition and has subsequently supported its realisation. His Grace the Duke of Devonshire, the Friends of the Towner, South East Arts Board, South East Museum Services and the Paul Mellon Centre for Studies in British Art have all been generous in their support. I am also pleased to acknowledge the sponsorship of the following local companies, individuals and organisations: Herrington's Solicitors, Honey Barrett, Maureen Honey, Mr & Mrs G. Household, the Association of Eastbourne Artists, the Eastbourne Club of Business and Professional Women and the Eastbourne Decorative and Fine Art Society.

Finally, it has been a pleasure to work with Hilary Lane, whose understanding of and insight into William Nicholson's painting has resulted in a rich and memorable exhibition. Her analysis of William Nicholson's painting in her catalogue essay is an invaluable contribution to the knowledge of his work. I hope that visitors to the Towner Art Gallery and the subsequent venues at Cambridge, Nottingham and London will enjoy looking at the exhibition as much as we enjoyed organising it.

Photograph of William Nicholson by Arburthnot, 1912.

Foreword

A few thoughts on being with my father, William Nicholson

Elizabeth Banks

This exhibition of landscapes and still lifes shows the work my father liked doing almost best of all; uncommissioned work, work he could do as if he were playing a game with the view, with the flowers in mugs and jugs, with the lights and shades, shapes and spaces, in the same way as he played tennis - as if the landscape or still life were bouncing back and playing ball with him.

He liked to bring this same energy to everything he did: playing at his work and working at his play - tennis, squash, croquet, throwing a boomerang, playing cup-and-ball - moving like a dancer trying out new steps, practising, exploring, entertaining, showing off. Winning was not so important because he loved to watch the way one could make the ball do unexpected, tricky things, and to have an amusing opponent to share the joke with.

Early days in Sutton Veny started in his little snuff-coloured room nestling in bed with Father - all close and cosy - he in his camel hair dressing gown having "no breakfast - just a boiled egg and a cup of coffee." He would give me the hat off his egg, carefully salted and peppered as a treat, then chatting and drawing as he talked - you never knew what was going to appear - 'blokes' and rabbits, lots of them, drawn all in one line.

He moved all the time, very agile, with the hands of a conjurer - sensitive, soft, supple, loose-skinned, square nails ingrained with paint. Doing naughty things at meals - drawing on the table cloth, balancing glasses on top of each other, skimming coloured raffia place-mats across the room. As a child I adored all this naughtiness and meal times were full of laughter, puns and stories.

Sometimes Father would put his paintbox in his green MG and we would make for the Downs, walk for miles looking at everything, excitedly finding plovers' nests and secret larks' nests or new mushrooms in the wet grass. Or he would sit with his paintbox at his knee (the panel board on which he painted fitted in its lid) his mouth watering as he laid the paint on - breathing hard with a wet cigarette hanging from his mouth - holding his breath from excitement of effort as he painted a specially succulent or difficult stroke.

Wandering in the garden we picked flowers for the house and many of these had to sit for him. Father jokingly claimed sweet williams were named after him. Butterflies seemed to love his smell - bay rum, turpentine, Balkan Sobranie cigarettes - and sometimes settled on his shirt.

Paint was food to him, his mouth watered as he laid it on with brush, sometimes the wrong end, and palette knife and thumb - a sensuous meal of taste and savour; in the same vein was his love of a perfectly cooked herring (always 'unbuttoned' with two forks), a humble subject with a little mustard and the right wine.

30
Sunfish 1935
Photo: Arts Council Collection

33
Cyclamen
1937

William Nicholson

Lillian Browse

I do not exactly remember when it was that I first met William Nicholson but I believe it to have been towards the late thirties when he would have been approaching his sixty-fifth year. He was one of those rare people whom it seemed "Age could not wither...", on the contrary, I felt that he must have grown more delightful as the years progressed.

The circumstances of our meeting are amusing to recall because, at the time, I was a novitiate art dealer at Leger's Old Master Gallery, in Old Bond Street, where I had been allowed the use of one floor in which to make contemporary exhibitions. As a change from a series of one-man shows I had decided to try a theme. How I came to choose Nudes as a subject for this innovation I cannot imagine for Nudes were 'shocking' and totally unsaleable, only acceptable as hung at the Royal Academy. However I drew up a list of the best known British artists not knowing whether they painted the Nude or not and the fact that my list included William Nicholson's name was evidence of my more than slender knowledge.

Without giving any reason I wrote to Mr Nicholson asking whether I could have an appointment and, much to my surprise, was invited to Apple Tree Yard, his entrancing studio/home, whose address has become almost legendary. And entrancing it was with its Vermeer-like interior, its same air of calm, its black and white chequered floor and its angle of light flooding through the tall window illuminating the bric-a-brac on the Regency table. This bric-a-brac comprised a top hat in which Nicholson kept his brushes - some worn down to the ferrule; jugs of all sorts from his cherished collection; women's long suede evening gloves in a variety of hues - the last flickering of elegance, and bilboquets and a globe of the world. The top hat had belonged to Max Beerbohm; the window had been designed by Lutyens. The whole imparted a feeling of workman-like fastidiousness whose owner was accustomed to quality in all that he possessed.

The artist had been working in his normal attire - immaculate white trousers, pink-spotted white shirt with butterfly collar, bow tie, lemon socks and patent leather shoes - certainly a dandy but never pretentious. Despite my surprise and nervousness I was almost immediately put at my ease because I was received with such charming courtesy as might have been extended to someone of real importance. However surprised Nicholson might have been at my request for a Nude, his beautiful manners did not allow him to show anything other than serious consideration. As it happened he had one in his studio which was brought forth from behind a stack of canvases. It could not have differed more from the seductive, golden-haired, vapidly pretty girl by Wilfred de Glehn R.A. which I had already secured and which, at that stage of my career, I greatly admired. The Nicholson Nude was of a very plain woman lying flat on her back and looking for all the world as if a steam-roller had run over her. But it was a Nicholson; he was willing to lend it and I could not have been more thrilled.

During my visit a man-servant, carrying a tea-tray, appeared through the floor as if by pantomime magic; he came through a trap-door from the kitchen below with all the solemnity of a professional butler opening the doors of some splendid salon. This 'magical' act tickled Nicholson's sense of humour, an element of the boyishness he ever retained. No wonder he was loved by all who knew him, and so attractive to those who were merely acquaintances.

After this first and brief encounter I was not to be in touch with William Nicholson again until the middle of the war, when I was organising the war-time exhibitions at the National Gallery. By this time he was living with the writer, Marguerite Steen in Bruton Street and I remember being enormously impressed by the name-plate on the door which read "William Nicholson and Marguerite Steen". So frank an acknowledgement of 'living in sin' was more than unusual in those non-permissive days.

In 1942 when the bombing had become too fierce and the National Gallery had sustained several hits, we moved to the smaller galleries on the ground floor where we decided to twin the Irish Jack Yeats with William Nicholson, both of whom had started in 'publicity' but had then developed in extremely divergent ways. As Nicholson was a close friend of the Churchills,

Sir Kenneth Clark had organised a lunch in the gallery to celebrate the exhibition's opening at which Lady Churchill was to be the guest of honour. Neither Marguerite Steen nor I, the organiser, had been invited and William was so incensed at this insult to us both that he vowed he would not attend either. Ten minutes before lunch was due to begin he could not be found anywhere – he was actually hiding in one of the Gallery's small rooms trying to improve upon a painting. No persuasion would induce him to budge. Sir Kenneth was forced to swallow his pride and asked if I could help. I suggested to William that his absence would constitute an unforgivable insult to 'Clemmie' and that Marguerite and I would have a 'binge' on our own so he grudgingly succumbed and to everybody's relief went to the lunch.

After the war and with the advent of Roland, Browse and Delbanco, William Nicholson became one of our gallery artists, and such was his lack of interest in money that he was shocked when we found it necessary to double his prices which, even in those times of extreme modesty, were ridiculously low. Whenever we had any of his pictures hanging I tried to accompany him as he walked around the gallery, this was because he had the habit of picking hair-pins off the pavement, stuffing them in his pocket and using them to scratch any small adjustment he thought necessary to one of his works. I dissuaded him whenever I could.

William Nicholson was far from being an intellectual painter, on the contrary he was an artist whose response was awakened by such as the appeal of a Downland landscape or an uncluttered still life. Sophisticated simplicity informs his best work to such an extent that before a small painting of a jug or distant hills one is deceived into murmuring "What is all the fuss about – it looks so easy". A small master from the stream of classic art that has run through the centuries and is today so unfashionable, Nicholson cultivated a refined sense of tonality and indulged in a controlled enjoyment of the handling of oil paint, that luscious pigment today so abused. His famous son's passionless but fastidious geometric compositions with their even, flat surfaces were quite beyond his father's comprehension and led William to exclaim "I don't know what has happened to Ben, he used to paint so nicely".

1

Still Life 1907

2

Fuchsias in a Blue and White Jug 1909

3

Viola on the Downs 1909

4

The Windmill,
Brighton Downs 1910

5

A Downland Scene
1910

7
Brighton Downs, Early Morning 1910

11
Devil's Flight, Gloucestershire c.1911

6

The Ruby Glass 1910

8

The Lowestoft Bowl 1911

Photo: Tate Gallery, London

9
Sea and Sky 1911

12
Judd's Farm 1912

10

Tulips and Bowl 1911

13
White Tulips 1912

21
Cliffs at Rottingdean
c.1923

15
*The Hill above
Harlech* c.1917
Photo: Tate Gallery,
London

14
Whiteways, Evening 1913

17
The Lustre Casket 1920

26

Mixed Flowers in a Jug 1929

19
Hilder's Patch 1921

Looking Through the Paintings

Hilary Lane

In 1993, The Towner Art Gallery, Eastbourne and Hove Museum and Art Gallery organised an ambitious exhibition *The Sussex Scene*. This brought together work by the many artists who have found the Sussex landscape an inspiration for, and the subject of, their work. For me, one small painting expressed more than any other the experience of the Sussex landscape. *Hilder's Patch* (cat.19) was so direct it seemed almost to have been thought on to the canvas. There is no obvious technique, point of view, or manner of expression. The personality of the artist does not interpose between the viewer's experience of the painting and the landscape itself. The great pleasure this gives, of course, is that we seem to be painting or seeing the picture ourselves, rather than wondering at the skill of the artist or conjecturing about how it was done. This clarity of seeing then stays with us and turns the view of the landscape that we see from the train window on the way home into paintings.

At this point I knew very little about William Nicholson apart from his connection with Rottingdean, his black and white woodcuts and illustrations for books. I knew of his reputation as a portrait painter. But I had seen *Sunfish* (cat.30) and *Pears* (cat.35) which together with *Hilder's Patch* offered the promise that an exhibition of still life and landscape painting could be made and would reveal William Nicholson's particular qualities as a painter. The time seemed right for such an exhibition. In a world where the challenges and manifestations of art are many and various, the idea that it is possible to recreate or pin down some of the world we see around us in pigment and oil on a flat board remains a wonder in itself. William Nicholson's paintings do not attempt to do more, except perhaps to convey his pleasure in both what he is painting and his ability to paint it. He did not approach his painting in an intellectual or theoretical way, he very rarely responded to requests to write about it or make statements. He said 'it is difficult to rebuild in words what one records in paint'[1] and, he might have added, pointless too.

This selection of paintings, which is a personal one, was made in that spirit; not to make an art historical point or to illustrate a theory. Rather the hope has been to make an exhibition in which the paintings could communicate directly. There could and I hope will be, many other exhibitions of William Nicholson's work. Even one which was restricted, as this is, to still life and landscape could look very different. William Nicholson's son Ben, writing after his father's death said "In my opinion Father's work reputation will increase year by year on the basis 1. of his still lifes and 2. of his poetic landscapes."[2]

How did William Nicholson achieve such directness, how did he think paintings on to canvas? His biographer and last companion Marguerite Steen, mentions that he always seemed to start a painting just as they were about to leave a place where they had been staying for several weeks. William Nicholson had to know somewhere before he could paint it, he also had to want to paint it. He had to see and to know something very particular about the motif before he could start. It was for this reason that he often found formal portraiture a trial.

This process of observation is like being in love; seeing and knowing with tenderness. He would leave a still life subject arranged and untouched for days before painting it. The more closely something is observed the more lovely it becomes. He also spent time looking at a blank canvas hanging at the foot of his bed, so he knew both the subject and the space it was to occupy. After seeing and knowing, came painting, which he did with technical expertise. He painted very swiftly and with great skill, often at one go. Then it was the next thing that was important. However when he describes painting *Judd's Farm* (cat.12) and says "I could finish it in my head before releasing the paint" he describes that as a "rare experience",[1] so it would be a mistake to imagine that the realisation of his vision always came easily, or somehow spontaneously. He could analyse his technique and knew how and why he used a certain tonal range. But he liked company when he worked and could paint in the middle of family life, as if he needed to disengage part of his attention from the process.

That the quality of tenderness towards what is being painted was important for William Nicholson is made clear in the paintings themselves and is borne out in a remark he made about painting a portrait of Sidney and Beatrice Webb. They are seen in front of a large, plain, brick fireplace. He wrote "The problem of painting the two hundred bricks as though you loved them is a solemn thought… I had to forget they were bricks and think of them as colour."[3]

Quite soon I noticed that in many of the paintings, both still life and landscape, a very satisfying ellipse was central to the composition. Later in other paintings I identified what I thought of as a fish shape.

An ellipse is very difficult to render with conviction and clearly William Nicholson enjoyed the shape very much and was good at painting it convincingly. The problem with an ellipse is the huge distance from front to back, which of course equals the width. This distance has to be compressed, the more so at what become the right and left edges, whilst maintaining the continuity of the rim. William Nicholson had clearly observed many such ellipses; the rims of cups and bowls and plates, viewed almost from above in *The Little Flower Piece* (cat.20) and *The Bull-ring, Malaga* (cat.29) or almost level in *Still Life* (cat.1). It seemed to me that he had especially enjoyed these observations and knew the translation of a circle to an ellipse very well. It was pleasing to discover that he enjoyed playing with a cup-and-ball and was very skilful and adept with it. Although his own mahogany bilboquet was heavy he made a point of travelling with it. He had therefore seen the ball fall satisfactorily into the cup thousands of times and many of his compositions echo this. The composition of the painting falls into the ellipse in a satisfying way. In the early *Still Life*, the brown tea-pot, blue enamel mug and pink rimmed plates sit in the dark shadow. In *Judd's Farm* there is a curve in the landscape in which the buildings sit.

William Nicholson could flick a playing card in such a way that it would fly through the air and return to him. He also had a boomerang whose flight he enjoyed. The same pleasure of flight and return is evident in the composition of the paintings. The fish shape which occupies the area below the horizon line in *Scratchbury in Snow* (cat.24) for example - the boomerang at its furthest point; or describing a curve, as in *Snow in the Horseshoe* (cat.25); or having come to rest in *The Silver Casket* (cat.16). Here the casket is placed far back so it can occupy a space high up on the canvas, leaving room for the curving shapes of beads and gloves to land. *The Lustre Casket* (cat.17) is held aloft on a red shoe box with curving echoes in the pattern on the casket and the cloth. In *Lowestoft Bowl* (cat.8) one ellipse is caught in another, one light and one dark, set against a black background.

Many amateur painters, painters for pleasure, share the subject matter of these pictures by William Nicholson. Their scale is familiar too; he often painted on a board which fitted into the top of his paintbox. He had a sympathy for the amateur painter and was very touched when the actor Joseph Jefferson, whose portrait he was painting in America, showed him his watercolours. He also gave Sir Winston Churchill painting lessons while staying at Chartwell. They often sat and painted side by side. Although a painter of his time and one who had learnt from the painters of the past, William Nicholson's paintings refer first to nature and not to other paintings. The amateur who might be thought to be attempting a similar task, often has the idea of a painting, which comes not from nature, but from the notion of a picture in mind. Paintings in cartoons and illustrations often conform to similar patterns. Alongside the modern sculpture with a hole in it or the head with two noses, might hang a downland landscape with a windmill or a jug of flowers.

What are the lessons to be learnt by the amateur painter from William Nicholson's use of this modest scale and subject matter? We can take great delight, for example, in the way the newspaper on which the jug is standing in *Tall Pewter Jug* (cat.39) has been painted. It is not a trick, in the way that trompe l'oeil paintings are; made to a formula, which is designed to deceive us into believing the unbelievable. William Nicholson has seen the newspaper so clearly, as he has seen the jug and the reflections in it, that we accept wholeheartedly all its qualities. This clarity of vision has enabled him to convey the idea and presence of newspaper in an apparently deft way. For the amateur painter the lesson is not how to paint newspaper, rather it is how to see it so clearly that it can be painted.

May Morning in Apple Tree Yard (cat.27) is not a picture for which there was an existing model in the artist's mind. He conveys to us just what it was that struck him as he looked down into the yard from his studio; the pink of the stack, the leaping flames and the directions of the planks. In *The Shadow of the Tower La Rochelle* (cat.36), how lovely to be spared a painting of the tower itself and instead, to see the upright masts which have movement and colour. By making his paintings, although simplified, so particular he avoids the banal.

In *Sea and Sky* (cat.9) there is no horizon line, the sea and sky become one, but the sky curves back towards us. In *Beau Rivage, Beau Matin* (cat.23) sea and sky meet on a slightly curved horizon. There seems no difference in the way the sea and the sky have been painted, the colour and the application of the paint is the same but we can see the point where one changes into the other.

William Nicholson's delight in playing tennis was not to win but to "place the ball in an unexpected place."[4] Similarly a sense of balance is achieved in the paintings in unexpected ways. In spite of the mass of the flowers in *Cyclamen* (cat.33) and the weight of the colour tipping over to the left and forward, the jug does not tip over because we read the pattern on it, not as surface decoration but as the substance of the jug. The dark, dark red of the *The Ruby Glass* (cat.6) is made darker and redder by the blue shadows and black ribbon, and the near circle of the glass in *The Little Flower Piece* (cat.20) is held in space by the light sparkling from it.

William Nicholson's early work designing posters and woodcuts imposed a discipline of limitation which he relished, it also directed his attention to the qualities of representation in black and white and to how little was needed to convey meaning. He later wrote "Have you noticed how subconsciously grateful one feels to the masters for their simplification of line, tone and colour".[1]

Although his paintings are tonal, he uses black and white as colours in them. The black background and white cloth of *White Tulips* (cat.13) are not simply light and shade but colours in their own right, as much as the deep blue of the jug. In woodcuts, black and white are convincing as colours and are not used as tones. In his house at Rottingdean and at Apple Tree Yard he had black and white chequered floors laid, and enjoyed looking at objects against them; one can be seen in the background of *Sunfish* (cat.30). He took delight in white and painted the chalky landscapes of Sussex and Wiltshire, the dry heat of the harvest scratched into the surface of *Corn Stooks* (cat.28) against a white sky. He painted landscapes under snow, ice, silver and white flowers, creamy white reflections in *The Gold Jug* (cat.34) on and against a white background.

These are not paintings of action. The drama has been off-stage and abstract, the telling moments, those when the decision has been made where to place the horizon, where to allow the elements in a still life to come to rest and the discovery of how little needs to happen to hold a space together. In *Whiteways, Evening* (cat.14) the relationship between the foreground figure in white and the person with the plough in the distance serves to measure the space between them, rather as the train in *Scratchbury in Snow* (cat.24) running across the painting, defines the valley. Although William Nicholson's approach to painting was not an intellectual one, it was far from unaware, he knew very well what a painting was. His paintings aspired to become the equivalents of what they depict. The key to this was observation. He wrote to his son Ben in 1914 "Now if you want to be a great painter you must be able to draw anything and everything draw, draw only draw".[5] Drawing in practice is seeing and discovering. In 1934 he wrote that Faraday's diary entry "must learn to observe" was a maxim "as perfect for a painter as for the scientist"[1] In these generous paintings we are invited to join the artist in this process.

Footnotes

[1] William Nicholson *The Artist* June 1934

[2] Letter from Ben Nicholson to Marguerite Steen, 1953, William Nicholson Trust Archive

[3] Famous Artists No21 by the Editor *The Artist* September 1953

[4] William Nicholson Trust Archive

[5] William Nicholson Trust Archive

18
Welsh Bread 1920

20

The Little Flower Piece 1923

22
Lilies of the Valley c.1924

24

Scratchbury in Snow 1927

25
Snow in the Horseshoe 1928

27

May Morning in Apple Tree Yard 1931

28
Corn Stooks c.1934

29
The Bull-ring, Malaga 1935
Photo: Tate Gallery, London

31
The Road to Zamaramala 1936

34
The Gold Jug 1937

32

Pink Still Life with Jug 1936

Photo: Published by permission of Birmingham Museums & Art Gallery

37
Silver c.1938
Photo: Tate Gallery, London

35

Pears 1938

Photo: Leeds City Art Galleries

38
Ciboure 1938

36

The Shadow of the Tower, La Rochelle 1938

39

Tall Pewter Jug 1939

40
Snow at Bretton Park 1939/40

41
Begonias 1939/40

42

Mushrooms 1940

Photo: Tate Gallery, London

23

Beau Rivage, Beau Matin 1926

The Career of William Nicholson

Patricia Reed

This exhibition makes no claim to be a representative selection of William Nicholson's work, rather it is personal selection by Hilary Lane, so a brief outline of the artist's career may be useful. Nicholson's work can be divided into four periods. During the first period in the 1890s he produced revolutionary posters as one of the Beggarstaff Brothers and woodcuts that were admired in countries as far away as Russia and America. Between 1901-40, when he was mainly engaged on portraiture, landscape and still life, three periods can be distinguished. In the years leading up to 1914 Nicholson's career as a society portrait painter was firmly established and he also became known for landscapes and still lifes with rich, dark backgrounds. There followed a period of transition and experiment, especially in still lifes, between 1915-20 when he briefly visited India and then experienced the tragedies and disruption of the First World War. After 1920 Nicholson abandoned his sombre palette, his still lifes became simpler and he found new landscape subjects in Spain and France. His achievements, especially in portraiture, were recognised by a knighthood in 1936.

Nicholson's dislike of publicity, the Royal Academy and of being associated with any particular school of painting are perhaps reasons why he is less well-known today than his friends and contemporaries William Orpen (1878-1931) and Augustus John (1878-1961). Always impeccably dressed, even when painting, Nicholson was elegant, fastidious, and sociable; a raconteur of the Café Royal generation with a particular sense of humour. At the same time he was a very energetic and hardworking man who took his work as an artist very seriously indeed.

Nicholson is often described as "a painter's painter", for his primary concern was the craft of painting and the possibilities of paint. In this he is like Manet, an artist with whom he has much in common. Nicholson's approach was painterly rather then linear, and he was always experimental in his technique. After 1920 his palette lightened dramatically but throughout his life Nicholson was always a tonal painter, a legacy from Whistler. He was also a realist, both in his painting and his approach to life, free of theories and ideology. Like Whistler, he believed in the importance of good taste and restraint. This attitude, combined with a strong sense of design and the ability to convey the essential qualities of a subject through a simplification of the image, is apparent in all his work, whether posters, paintings or woodcuts.

Although in later years Nicholson was to describe himself as self-taught, it can be argued that he gained from his two-year stay at Hubert von Herkomer's school his experimental approach to media and technique. There he also met his future wife, Mabel and her brother, the artist James Pryde. After their marriage in 1893 Nicholson set up with his brother-in-law as poster designers under the name of J & W Beggarstaff. From 1896 Nicholson worked on his own producing woodcuts, founding his career on the celebrated "Walking Tea-cosy" portrait of Queen Victoria, a realistic depiction of the elderly queen enlivened by humour and affection. He became a contributor of portraits to W.E. Henley's *New Review*, and within a few years produced a number of illustrated books that were widely popular, beginning with *The Alphabet* and *Almanac of Sports* for which Kipling wrote the verses. Throughout his life he enjoyed the company of poets, preferring them to painters. In the 1890s he was linked with the 'hearties' rather than the 'aesthetes' and the Englishness of his early subjects is perhaps a reflection of this; not just the coster girls, a popular subject with his contemporaries, but in his series of morris dancing paintings of 1901-07.

Nicholson's income was derived mainly from portraiture which occupied much of his time until 1940, when illness forced him to stop work. This was from necessity rather than choice. From the age of twenty-one he had people financially dependent on him: his wife and their four children, his daughter Nancy Nicholson and her husband, the poet Robert Graves, and their children during the 1920s and '30s (especially after the breakup of the marriage), and also in the 1930s when he was giving an allowance to his son Ben, who was making a career as an artist. Throughout his life Nicholson was surrounded by artists: his first wife Mabel was a talented painter who was beginning to make a name for herself when the First World War broke out.

After her death in 1918 he lost contact with her brother, James Pryde, but soon found himself amidst a second generation of artists. His second wife, Edie, painted under the name of Elizabeth Drury, Ben's first wife Winifred was also a painter (all three were members of the '7 and 5 Society'), and Nicholson's daughter Nancy and his son Kit's wife, E.Q., were designers. These contacts undoubtedly had an effect on his work.

Nicholson's woodcut portraits had demonstrated his ability to capture a likeness and made him known to a wide audience, but a realist with a sense of humour is not best suited to be a successful society portrait painter. He could not, or would not glamorise his sitters, partly because he was unable to take them as seriously as they did themselves, and if he felt unsympathetic towards a sitter, usually male, an element of caricature might slip in. Nicholson found children and women more congenial sitters, and produced some very perceptive and unsentimental portraits: *The Paper Cap* 1906 (private collection on loan to Nottingham Castle Museum and Art Gallery), *The Girl with the Tattered Glove* 1909 (Fitzwilliam Museum, Cambridge) and *Gertrude Jekyll* 1920 (National Portrait Gallery). It was a request for a child portrait in 1905 that introduced him to his most important patron, T.W. Bacon, who was to be a loyal supporter until the early 1920s. In his later years Nicholson's portraits of male sitters become more assured: among his finest are the artist *Walter Greaves* 1917 (Manchester City Art Gallery) and *The Earl of Harewood* 1936-37 (Freemasons Hall, London).

Some of Nicholson's best work was on a small scale. *The McKenna Boys* (The Museum, Eton College) for instance, though full-length is only 106.7 by 73.7cms. Successful large scale works were only achieved with tremendous effort, as was *Lord Hardinge, Viceroy of India* painted in India in 1915. Another work, which like *Lord Hardinge* was never exhibited in England, is his largest canvas (243.8 x 289.6cms) *The Canadian Headquarters Staff* 1918-19 (Canadian War Museum, Ottawa) painted for the Canadian War Memorials Committee and one of his few group portraits.

Landscapes and still lifes were a release from the grind of portraiture. Yet since he could ask £600 for a full-length portrait and only £50-£150 for a landscape in the 1910s and '20s they were also an indulgence. While major portrait commissions could take months, sometimes years to complete, landscapes were produced in a matter of hours, working on the spot and using the canvas boards that fitted into the lid of his paint box. Nicholson loved the calm empty expanses of the Downlands after the bustle and noise of his busy studio, filled with visitors, sitters and children for, paradoxically, he was an artist who enjoyed company when working. Many portraits were painted in the sitters' homes away from London and Nicholson was a welcome country house guest, always ready to entertain as well as be entertained. Landscapes, and often still lifes, were painted for relaxation during the portrait commission. For example *Snow at Bretton Park* (cat.40) and *Begonias* (cat.41) were painted during the long winter of 1939, part of which Nicholson spent working on Lord Allendale's portrait at his home in Yorkshire. The artist wrote to his daughter Elizabeth "my very latest still life painted with an urge in an all night sitting after a perfect dinner (O! the wine) at Bretton Park, home of Lord Allendale…"

Still lifes are Nicholson's most personal works. Early subjects are pieces of silver and ceramics, especially lustreware, much of it from his own collection. He chose them for the beauty of their form rather than with the eye of a connoisseur, and he did not set out to record them as objects. They presented the challenge of depicting reflective surfaces which was an inspiration to him until 1920. Generally the objects are set within a shallow picture space where the lighting creates strong shadows as part of the composition, and there is a strong horizontal emphasis. From 1910 Nicholson moved from the single object to two or three, arranged with conspicuous taste, as in *The Lowestoft Bowl* (cat.8) the first of Nicholson's paintings to enter a public collection.

The composition of still lifes with a large number of objects created the same problems for Nicholson as group portraiture, his imaginative powers being less well developed than his powers of observation and technical skills. In some early works the viewer may be forgiven for thinking that the objects have been chosen merely because they are difficult to paint. However he found inspiration in Spanish still life painting. In a group of large still lifes produced during the period 1914-18 Nicholson has replaced the allegory of Spanish still life with sentimental associations. Thus in *Studio Still Life* 1914 (Tate Gallery) measuring 132.1 by 162.6cms, the objects all have connections with his friend, the playwright Edward Knoblock in Paris, and in *Henley's Hat* 1917 (untraced) every object recalls the dead poet. One of his most popular pictures was painted at this time, *The Hundred Jugs* 1916 (Walker Art Gallery, Liverpool), as the result of a bet with his son Ben. Here Nicholson has extended his usual shallow picture space in order to include one hundred jugs, and a kitten. These more complex works were undoubtedly an attempt to come to terms with the War, at a time when he had largely abandoned landscape and had trouble completing portraits. They can also be linked with the trompe l'oeil murals that Nicholson was painting in the dining room at Folly Farm, Berkshire between 1916-19.

The period 1917-20 can be seen as a turning point in Nicholson's still lifes. Thereafter it seems as if he no longer needed to make large complex compositions, or to attempt references beyond the simple subjects he painted. His palette lightened and increasingly his interest focused on the surface texture of the painting, rather than on producing a virtuoso rendering of the surface of the object. The same experimental approach is present in his landscapes. The variety is exciting: from the economically painted *Little Flower Piece* 1923 (cat.20), the near abstraction of *Glass Jug and Fruit* 1938 (National Gallery of Canada, Ottawa) with thinly applied paint on very coarse canvas to *Flowers in Glass Vase* (Kirkcaldy), where the form is incised with a paintbrush end into the impastoed paint. A shallow picture space is still common but sometimes the horizontal emphasis is altered to a diagonal. New compositional devices such as placing objects on a pile of books from 1916, or set against a background of his sketches as in *The Gold Jug 1937* (cat.34) combine with earlier features such as the inclusion of truncated plates or knives to give depth to the picture space. Dating from the mid '20s to early '30s are an accomplished group of flower pieces that share steeply tilted picture planes, with different surface textures forming decorative patterns and incorporating the familiar shadow patterns, for example *Mauve Primulas on a Table* 1928 (Metropolitan Museum, New York).

Nicholson maintained the image of a dandy of the 1890s until his death in 1949. This image had perhaps obscured the experimental aspect of his work, which was certainly overlooked by the obituary writers who commented that Nicholson had been unambitious in his aims but what he did, he did extremely well. What he aimed for was a completely impartial recording of reality in terms of tone and colour; in this sense he was a realist and one for whom it could be argued that ultimately the subject did not matter. Yet it is through this impartial recording that his best works release the 'poetic' spirit, as his son Ben called it, a poetry inherent in the subjects themselves, whether landscape, still life or the individual.

Chronology – Sir William Nicholson

1872	5 February born at Newark, Nottinghamshire.
1889-91	Attends Hubert von Herkomer's art school at Bushey where he meets his future wife, Mabel Pryde, and her elder brother the artist James Pryde.
1891	Autumn in Paris where enrols for two weeks at the Académie Julian.
1893	Marries Mabel Pryde.
1894	First son, Ben, born.
1894-97	Works with brother-in-law James Pryde as J & W Beggarstaff producing posters.
1897	Second son, Anthony, born. First visit to Rottingdean, Sussex to make a portrait of Rudyard Kipling for *New Review*.
1897-1903	Lives at Chaucer's House, Woodstock.
1897-1900	Produces woodcut portraits and illustrated books which achieve widespread popularity.
1899	First daughter, Nancy, born.
1900	Wins gold medal at the Paris Exposition Universelle for his woodcuts, but has already decided to make his career as a painter.
1902	Visits New York to make portraits for Harper's Magazine.
1903	First solo show at the Stafford Gallery.
1904	The family move to Hampstead. Third son, Christopher, born.
1906	Career as a portrait painter firmly established with the success of 'Mrs Curle' at the International Society.
1909	Takes studio in The Pheasantry, Kings Road, Chelsea; buys the former vicarage at Rottingdean and renames it The Grange.
1914	Departs for India to paint the portrait of the Viceroy, Lord Hardinge.
1915	Returns to England. Mabel and the family at Harlech in Wales.
1917	Acquires studio at 11 Apple Tree Yard, St James's, his London home and studio until 1940.
1918	Death of his wife Mabel from influenza and of his son Tony on active service in France.
1919	Collaborates with his son-in-law, the poet Robert Graves, on an illustrated literary journal 'The Owl' (three issues). Marries a family friend, the painter Edith Stuart-Wortley (née Phillips), a war-widow with two small children. Winter in the South of France.
1920	Second daughter, Elizabeth, born in Wales. The family move to North End House, Rottingdean, Burne-Jones' former home.
1923	Moves to Sutton Veny, Wiltshire. Painting trips abroad during next decade include Avignon (1925), Brittany (1926) and Ireland (1931).
1933	Separates from his wife, house at Sutton Veny sold. Major retrospective at Nottingham, smaller version tours.
1934-39	A Trustee of the Tate Gallery.
1935	Visits Malaga, Spain where he meets the novelist Marguerite Steen; they live together until his death.
1936	Spring in Spain. Knighted in July.
1938	Spring in France, returns in autumn and spends six months mainly in La Rochelle.
1940	October leaves Apple Tree Yard studio during the Blitz. He ceases painting due to illness.
1942	Exhibition at The National Gallery with Jack Yeats.
1949	16 May dies, Blewbury, Berkshire.

Artists' Responses

Patrick Caulfield

Patrick George

Merlin James

Isobel Johnstone

Patrick Caulfield

Patrick Caulfield
Glass of Whisky 1987
acrylic on canvas
76.2 x 111.7
Saatchi Collection

The still lifes of William Nicholson have a fluent shorthand of brushwork that skillfully conveys highlight, reflection and sense of material, reminiscent of Manet's economy of means. This virtuosity comes together to create a convincing weight and reality. Add to this the restrained simplicity of composition and you have both vigour and monumentality in what are modest scale paintings.

My simple empathy with his work is one of, the anyway, common currency of still life painting: the depiction of timeless familiar objects, jugs, vases etc. Objects unexaggerated in scale. They are left solely with their own drama, described and enlightened by light and shade.

Patrick George

Tall Pewter Jug (cat.39) is a serious and sombre still life. A grey shiny jug, possibly a claret jug, stands on some folded newspapers: the white and grey of the newspapers relieved by a strange subdued pink, the background is khaki. The year is 1939. Was it the outbreak of the war that gave rise to these sombre colours? If the colour of the objects and the colours they are painted is subdued, the shapes are certainly not. The shapes wriggle and twist with a strange life of their own. The idea is clear: to paint a shiny pewter jug. The shapes found in the jug are unpredictable, they have their particularity of shape and colour and texture. The highlight on the swelling of the jug is inordinately rough with dry, thick, white paint, into it is set a thin cool grey flame-like shape, around and below are the darker colours with a soft long undulating shape like the bedclothes of an unmade bed, stretching from side to side of the jug. Up the side, past the handle, are several long writhing flame-like shapes. To their side and below, the cast shadow on the newspaper has a shape like the tentacles of a sea creature. These shapes in themselves, evocative of living things, together form a description of an inanimate object. The newspaper serves as a foil to the jug, the paint, laid on with a palette knife, forms a strange

Patrick George
Trees, Sky and Pond
oil on canvas,
113.7 x 127.3

corrugated surface and some of the photographs in the paper, and particularly the three forked shadows within the fold, echo the living shapes within the jug.

Years ago in the art school at Edinburgh, there was a course in still life painting run by Mr MacTaggart. The students were given objects to paint placed in an artificial corner setting. The objects were chosen for their difference in shape and size and material; there were shiny pottery jugs, plates and glasses, small boxes and various strips of brightly coloured material. The students had to render these differences as best they could. This course, like the other courses in the school, was following an old tradition of teaching and more than likely a tradition that came from Paris. With the Impressionists and their belief in the all overness of light, the interest in particular textures disappeared. William Nicholson seems to have re-invented the subject of texture in still life. He relishes in the sparkling of silver, the glow of copper, the glisten of porcelain and the crumple of newspaper. Painting once again becomes alchemy and we marvel how the pigment is transformed.

The paintings of landscapes were all done outside straight from the view. The earlier landscape paintings of the Downs have a bland simplicity. More often than not the canvas is divided into equal parts of sky and land. The sky without clouds, perhaps an evening sky and as a pale shape it presses hard on the sweeping skyline of the Downs. The land is all brownish, really a darker version of the sky and this all over warm brown shape presses upwards to support the sky. The strength of the picture is in this meeting of sky and land, or the edge to edge of a pale shape and a brownish warm shape. There is considerable beauty in the strong abstract tension which varies in intensity along its length but always remains absolutely clear.

Like the still lifes, the landscapes are translations into swishy translucent oily brush strokes. The skilful strokes stand for sky and land but also for an exhibition of 'belle peinture'. You recognise the deftness of the brush stroke that is at the same time a tree or a bush. There is a seascape with boats, slipped in with a full brush, that makes a rhythm of dots and dashes like exclamation marks across the surface. You enter into the artist's response to his subject so that the picture is not just a plain statement of fact but a picture of the artist painting the object. These are exhilarating virtuoso performances where there can be no second thoughts, apparently no rubbing out and the little pictures almost certainly completed in one sitting.

Merlin James

Merlin James
Ruin 1995
acrylic on canvas
55.8 x 76.2
Courtesy of
Reed's Wharf
Gallery, London

It is easy to underestimate William Nicholson's domestic still lifes and atmospheric landscapes. Especially now, after recent burlesque neo-expressionism and 'issue-aware' neo-conceptualism, they might appear small fry.

His style was never radical. It derives from Velázquez, Chardin, Corot and Manet. Also Whistler, though Nicholson is far more telling than him in relating the tone and hue of sky to water below, or handling ineffable horizons and transitions. Whistler by comparison relies on a general sense of sensibility and stylistic felicity.

While as a graphic artist Nicholson had deployed dramatic black-and-white contrast, in oils he pursues tonal nuances - lights against lights, darks against darks, mid tones against mid tones. Similarly, he will combine textures and materials of similar rather than contrasting qualities - shiny silver with shiny pottery, matte petals with matte cloth. Analogously, in structuring pictures, he groups together all ovoid forms, or all ragged forms, or all angular forms, rather than creating obvious counterpoint.

Within his small scale, Nicholson does fascinating things with scale. Architecture becomes like still life - a distant bull-ring appearing like an ashtray. Conversely, a silver tray evokes moonlit water. These ambiguities result in a very understated surrealism. His mushrooms recall Paul Nash's looming biomorphic presences. Arguably Nicholson has more mystery, less mystification.

His painting is metaphoric, not least in its vestigial vanitas iconography of cut flowers, dead fish, polished surfaces soon to tarnish, and those transitory mushrooms. The delicate light of the paintings itself symbolises passing time.

The things represented are often artifacts, juxtaposed with nature - ornamental architecture in landscape, decorated ceramics containing fruit - suggesting a nature/art relationship. There is the particular thrill when he paints, say, the glazed pattern on a vase, and touches on the simultaneity of his own painting's artifice with that of the thing it depicts. In one picture he includes one of his own unfinished paintings as a backdrop: the very weave of *The Gold Jug's* rough canvas itself becomes a representation of the surface of the unfinished canvas depicted in the background (cat.34). This background picture, bearing the first notations of a recessive landscape, has its illusionism denied by the shadow of the 'genuinely' three-dimensional jug, and is also reflected in the jug, which reflects as well the painter's - viewer's - space, and, obscurely, a fugitive presence which must be that of the artist, the viewer.

But Nicholson does not invoke cliches of art's permanence and life's brevity. Rather he suggests that art, like everything, exists in passing time. Knives in his still lifes, which will slice fruit, bread, cake, frequently sink 'into' the paintings themselves, lost under the lips of plates or in shadows behind objects. A scissor that has cut flower stems will rest with its tips on the very edge of the canvas itself.

If there is a dated, 'period' feel to the Edwardian props and the conventional style, this is subsumed into the work's meaning. The candid historical specificity may be an advantage over art that aspires to more obvious transcendence. *The Lowestoft Bowl* (cat.8) sets up an emotive formal equation of tone and weight not unlike Rothko, or Ben Nicholson. But because their work is grandly ambitious, it is vulnerable to the accusation of being at base merely sentimental, dependent on trite associations (darkness with night, straight lines with horizons, diffusedness with cloud, circles with moons,etc.). William Nicholson, however, begins with the sentimentalised object - the dusk, the horizon, the cloud - and avoids sentimentality because he seems to explore the process whereby things, places, become the subject of our emotional and psychological projections. His work's poignancy and plangency seems again very conscious.

Human dramas, human feelings, are off-stage in the pictures. But the world of places and objects around us is perhaps only moving in relation to them; moving both in its capacity to carry associations, offer metaphors for the facts of our lives, and conversely in its very otherness - its being precisely not human life. Perhaps that is partly what Nicholson's very tacit paintings are about.

Isobel Johnstone

Isobel Johnstone
Badia a Passignano
1993
oil on canvas
21 x 25

It is a curious fact about paintings of nature that detail is death. Although we can spot every twig and spider in a Pre-Raphaelite picture it no more comes to life than a specimen pinned to a board. William Nicholson found most refreshment as a painter by immersing himself in nature but he did not allow detail to smother reality. Faced with its profusion he was able to simplify and at the same time to express his experience of a particular moment.

He learned about arrangement and colour harmony from Whistler and about the effectiveness of black and white from Velázquez and Manet. This knowledge was part of a repertoire of skills which as a true professional he practised lightly in a style expressive of a certain aristocratic nonchalance. Confidence in handling was part of his success as a portrait painter.

In its way landscape is as demanding as an eminent sitter and painting is like a performance involving initial nervousness and growing familiarity, with speed, an essential part of the process. Like other innovative artists, William Nicholson found that landscape and still life allowed more scope for self expression and formal experimentation. He did not go all the way to abstraction being rather too fond of his subject, especially the challenge of conveying movement which expressed the living heart of things. As a performer it might be said that he 'shared the bill' with nature, letting it take the lead and teach him to see the world afresh.

His landscapes are without the Edwardian undertones that linger in some of his still lifes. He responded to each encounter with the out-of-doors in a way that still rings true. Although I admire the way his loaded brush animates still life, I prefer his landscapes where sunshine and clouds dictate the bleached out harmonies and elicit unexpected gleams.

Catalogue

Measurements are given in centimetres, height before width. The 'B' reference in brackets at the end of most of the entries below denotes the catalogue number given by Lillian Browse in *William Nicholson* Rupert Hart-Davis, 1956.

1. *Still Life* 1907
Oil on canvas, 27.3 x 33.4
Private Collection
Illus p.14 (B.54)

2. *Fuchsias in a Blue and White Jug* 1909
Oil on canvas, 27.7 x 22.3
Private Collection
Illus p.15 (B.144)

3. *Viola on the Downs* 1909
Oil on canvas, 28.6 x 38.7
Private Collection
Illus p.16 (B.86)

4. *The Windmill, Brighton Downs* 1910
Oil on canvas, 33 x 40.6
City of Nottingham Museums, Castle Museum & Art Gallery
Illus p.17 (B.96)

5. *A Downland Scene* 1910
Oil on canvas, 33 x 40.6
Private Collection
Illus p.17

6. *The Ruby Glass* 1910
Oil on canvas board, 26.1 x 22.3
Private Collection
Illus p.20 (B.131)

7. *Brighton Downs, Early Morning* 1910
Oil on canvas board, 30.5 x 38.1
Private Collection
Illus p.18 (B.93)

8. *The Lowestoft Bowl* 1911
Oil on canvas, 47.5 x 61
Tate Gallery. Presented by the Contemporary Art Society in 1917.
Illus p.21 (B.137)

9. *Sea and Sky* 1911
Oil on canvas board, 31.1 x 38.7
Private Collection
Illus p.22 (B.105)

10. *Tulips and Bowl* 1911
Oil on canvas, 33 x 40
Private Collection
Illus p.24

11. *Devil's Flight, Gloucestershire* c.1911
Oil on canvas, 50.8 x 59.7
Sheffield City Art Galleries
Illus p.19 (B.109)

12. *Judd's Farm* 1912
Oil on canvas, 33 x 41
Private Collection
Illus p.23 (B.559)
Towner Art Gallery showing only.

13. *White Tulips* 1912
Oil on canvas, 58.4 x 53.4
His Grace the Duke of Devonshire
Illus p.25 (B.157)

14. *Whiteways, Evening* 1913
Oil on canvas, 55.9 x 60.9
Private Collection
Illus p.27 (B.121)

15. *The Hill above Harlech* c.1917
Oil on canvas, 53.7 x 59.4
Tate Gallery. Purchased with assistance from the Knapping Fund.
Illus p.26 (B.202)

16. *The Silver Casket* 1919
Oil on canvas, 33. x 40.7
Private Collection
Illus Cover (B.230)

17. *The Lustre Casket* 1920
Oil on canvas, 33 x 40.6
William Darby
Illus *p.28* (B.241)

18. *Welsh Bread* 1920
Oil on canvas, 50.5 x 50
Private Collection
Illus p.37 (B.360)
Towner Art Gallery and Browse & Darby showings only.

19. *Hilder's Patch* 1921
Oil on canvas, 52.1 x 57.2
Private Collection on loan to Nottingham Castle Museum and Art Gallery.
Illus p.30 (B.213)

20. *The Little Flower Piece* 1923
Oil on panel, 22.2 x 27.3
Private Collection
Illus p.38 (B.373)

21. *Cliffs at Rottingdean* c.1923
Oil on canvas, 36.8 x 45.7
Private Collection
Illus p.26 (B.92)

22. *Lilies of the Valley* c.1924
Oil on board, 38.1 x 29.2
Private Collection
Illus p.39 (B.376)
Towner Art Gallery and Browse &
Darby showings only.

23. *Beau Rivage, Beau Matin* 1926
Oil on panel, 38.1 x 45.7
Collection of Charles Bravington
Illus p.56 (B.328)

24. *Scratchbury in Snow* 1927
Oil on canvas on panel, 33 x 40.6
Private Collection
Illus p.40 (B.332)

25. *Snow in the Horseshoe* 1928
Oil on canvas board, 31.1 x 38.7
Private Collection
Illus p.41 (B.342)

26. *Mixed Flowers in a Jug* 1929
Oil on canvas, 33 x 40.7
Private Collection
Illus p.29 (B.393)

27. *May Morning in Apple Tree
Yard* 1931
Oil on canvas board, 32.4 x 40.6
Private Collection
Illus p.42 (B.351)

28. *Corn Stooks* c. 1934
Oil on canvas board, 36.8 x 45.7
Private Collection
Illus p.43 (B.315)

29. *The Bull-ring, Malaga* 1935
Oil on wood, 64.8 x 77.7
Tate Gallery. Presented by Miss H.
Stocks, 1989
Illus p.44 (B.454)

30. *Sunfish* 1935
Oil on canvas, 50.8 x 63.5
Arts Council Collection, the Hayward
Gallery, London
Illus p.9 (B.500)

31. *The Road to Zamaramala* 1936
Oil on canvas on wood, 30.5 x 40
Sheffield City Art Galleries
Illus p.45 (B.469)

32. *Pink Still Life with Jug* 1936
Oil on panel, 35.5 x 43.2
Birmingham Museums & Art Gallery
Illus p.47 (B.502)

33. *Cyclamen* 1937
Oil on panel, 39.4 x 31.8
Private Collection
Illus p.10 (B.519)
Towner Art Gallery and Browse &
Darby showings only.

34. *The Gold Jug* 1937
Oil on canvas board, 40.6 x 33
Her Majesty, Queen Elizabeth, The
Queen Mother.
Illus p.46 (B.505)

35. *Pears* 1938
Oil on canvas, 31.3 x 43.8
Leeds Museums & Galleries, City Art
Gallery.
Illus p.49 (B.507)

36. *The Shadow of the Tower, La
Rochelle* 1938
Oil on panel, 31.8 x 40
Private Collection
Illus p.51 (B.482)

37. *Silver* c.1938
Oil on board, 43.8 x 57.1
Tate Gallery. Purchased 1938.
Illus p.48 (B.509)

38. *Ciboure* 1938
Oil on canvas, 40.6 x 53.4
Private Collection
Illus p.50 (B.493)

39. *Tall Pewter Jug* 1939
Oil on canvas board, 45.7 x 39.4
Private Collection
Illus p.52 (B.510)

40. *Snow at Bretton Park* 1939/40
Oil on panel, 38.1 x 45.7
Private Collection
Illus p.53 (B.497)

41. *Begonias* 1939/40
Oil on canvas board, 40.6 x 47
Private Collection
Illus p.54 (B.525)
Towner Art Gallery and Browse &
Darby showings only.

42. *Mushrooms* 1940
Oil on canvas board, 34.9 x 45.1
Tate Gallery. Purchased 1941.
Illus p.55 (B.511)

Bibliography

1923   Kennedy North, S. *William Nicholson* Ernest Benn 1923

1943   Steen, Marguerite, *William Nicholson* Collins 1943

1948   Nichols, Robert *William Nicholson* Penguin Modern Painters 1948

1956   Browse, Lillian *William Nicholson* Rupert Hart-Davis 1956

1992   Campbell, Colin, *William Nicholson The Graphic Work* Barrie & Jenkins Ltd 1992

Selected Exhibitions
All held in London unless stated otherwise

1903   Stafford Gallery *The Works of William Nicholson*

1910   The Chenil Gallery *Exhibition of Paintings by William Nicholson*

1918   Goupil Gallery Summer Exhibition *Still Life etc by William Nicholson*

1927   Beaux Arts Gallery *Pictures and Drawings by William Nicholson*

1928   Alex. Reid and Lefevre (Glasgow) *Exhibition of Paintings by William Nicholson*

1929   Beaux Arts Gallery *Exhibition of Recent Paintings by William Nicholson*

1933   Nottingham Castle Museum and Art Gallery *Retrospective Exhibition of Paintings by William Nicholson*

          Beaux Arts Gallery *Retrospective Exhibition of Paintings by William Nicholson*

1934   Belfast Museum and Art Gallery *Loan Exhibition of Paintings and Prints by William Nicholson*

          Usher Art Gallery, Lincoln *Exhibition of Paintings and Lithographs by William Nicholson*

          Newark Municipal Museum *Exhibition of Paintings by William Nicholson*

1936   Leicester Galleries *Paintings by William Nicholson*

1938   Leicester Galleries *William Nicholson*

1943   Leicester Galleries *Paintings by Sir William Nicholson*

1947   Arts Council touring show *Sir William Nicholson Paintings, Woodcuts and Lithographs*

1967   Marlborough Fine Art *Sir William Nicholson*

1972   Roland, Browse and Delbanco *William Nicholson Centenary Exhibition*

1980   Arts Council touring show *William Nicholson Paintings, Drawings and Prints*

1990   Browse and Darby *William Nicholson 1872-1949*